For Greil —
Here's to
gifts of truth
Blessings,
Pamela

PRAISE FOR *HAIR ON FIRE*

Pamela Williams searches for beauty in unlikely places and shares the insights gleaned from a well-lived life. She knows both the risks and the opportunities of opening one's heart to the pain of the world, to loving it, and to forgiving oneself.

> —Barry Spector, author of *Madness at the Gates of the City: The Myth of American Innocence.*

Pamela Williams' poetry 'lulls and nudges' us to expand our interior lives. She beckons us to live a little longer inside ourselves before we speak or act. It's not that what we do or say will be altered by slowing down. But when we allow the tiniest exploration of more time and space within ourselves, we savor just how delicious it is our being alive. Read Williams to experience hesitation, the poetry of temporal and suspended states.

> —Dawn Sandoe, Writer

Unpretentious. Heartfelt. Vulnerable. Alive

When I read poetry I want the artist to take me on a journey, to guide and reveal things in depth. I want to be brought into the heart of the mystery and miracle with someone who knows the landscape and the language.

Pamela's artistry as a poet, guide and visionary, brings a felt sense of comfort, familiarity and curiosity that invites the reader to look beneath the surface of the seemingly simple relations of everyday life. With an immediate and artful approach to the mundane, her poetry offers us a new pair of glasses—a way of seeing new paths in old terrain; an invitation to risk empathic relatedness; a view of the often unnoticed creative interplay between people, objects, art and nature. All this comes through the simple act of attending to what's in front of you—observing, acknowledging and allowing.

At this time in history, we need poets of this caliber. So if you're looking for good poetry that takes you on that kind of connective journey, that reveals the soul and mysteries of everyday things, that maps the secret places of the heart, then I wholeheartedly suggest you pick up this treasure of a book and allow it to guide you to a new vision of unity and participation with the life about you.

> —Sofiah Ngoran
> Spiritual Life Coach & Teacher
> www.SpiritRx.net

I have always been an admirer of Pamela Williams's mid-Western wit and ability to turn a phrase. And now, from her southwestern village of Santa Fe, she takes a stand - as though in the company of a band of coyotes—releasing her lyrical Hair on Fire. Here, Pamela opens a metaphorically-forged gate for us to enter and to share her private landscape of carefully crafted observations. Once you enter and quietly settle into her world, you will be inspired to see that "the more vulnerable you are, the more invulnerable you are".

> —Charles Fox
> "Humanity is my family"

This girl's Hair is truly on fire! Whether she's climbing a mesa, roasting potatoes, or riffing on the "color blue," Pamela Williams is looking long & hard at Bedouin Carpets, Canyons, Apricots, and Cottonwoods, but even more closely at the ties that bind us or tear us apart. These poems are full of faith and irony, as in "The Journey" ...*you go along believing that you can see where the road is going in the distance, intention trumping logic once again.* Compassionate and challenging, Williams is "communing with the source," whether it be mice, prayers or peppermint, she takes the risk. Wily and optimistic, she embarks upon the Fools Journey, and brings us with her (knowing or not knowing) what might lie ahead. The Tower may be in flames but we are all *fugitive connecting threads* she *is knitting into her dreams.*

Bon Courage, I say, and thank you for taking us along for the ride.

—Ruthanne Martin, author of *Now, Voyager Celtic Faerie Tales* at magicaladventuresofvoyager.com; *Morning Glow: Reflections* with Stewart S. Warren; and her web presence: Abracadabra Tarot *–www. ramartin-rudy.blogspot.fr*

Mercury HeartLink
www.heartlink.com

Hair
on
Fire

Hair

on

Fire

PAMELA WILLIAMS

Hair on Fire: poems
Copyright ©2016 Pamela Williams

ISBN: 978-1-940769-62-2
Publisher: Mercury HeartLink
Silver City, New Mexico
Printed in the United States of America

Cover: from assemblage "Hair on Fire"
by Pamela Williams

Images for sections - details from assemblages
by Pamela Williams(in order):
'Altars'
'Balance, Some Disassembly Required'
'Receive'
'Dissection'
'Legacy'
'Hair on Fire'

Back cover photo of author by Lea Morales

Contact: pamelanow@yahoo.com

Hair on Fire

Altars

Balance

Receive

Dissection

Legacy

Hair on Fire

For Emily, Emmett, and Minette,
offering loving prayers that you
carry the pen and the brush forward,
along with a sense of
wonder and gratitude for all the mysteries
and magic on the journey.

INTRODUCTION

by Arnell Ando

Pamela Williams has a Renaissance curiosity about the world which illuminates all she gazes upon and it is with great pleasure that I write an introduction for this luminous poet. These are heartfelt, evocative pieces that speak in a meaningful way and I'm delighted to share my enthusiasm and acclaim.
I was fortunate to travel with Ms. Williams through Italy one cheery spring and have since come to know her as a big-hearted, self-aware artist and this wonderful collection reveals her talent. For she is able to tap into her inner beliefs and feelings and express them in ways that are both familiar and at times fresh and unexpected, while exploring the magnitude, singularity and permeability of our shared existence.

I remember warmly an evening she read a handful of poems so tenderly that it brought tears to my eyes. It is a special person who is able to achieve this and this collection is wonderful in allowing us to see her gift of observation and her willingness to perceive life's losses and the delicate offerings we so often miss.

Her work is both refreshingly original and heartwarmingly universal. The poem, Curious is especially touching, expressing time spent observing an inquisitive child, while mysterious occurrences in another room transpire.

And one can perhaps relate, as I do, to celestial ponderings in *Choices*:

>Overwhelmed, some days.
>Which sage to read, and meditate upon.
>What path the cards align.
>and the looming force of the planets...

And the heartbreak and raw emotion of **My Own Benabbio** softly shares with tender vulnerability.

Williams writes in such a way that we feel entranced to explore with her. In the poem, *Gaia Receiving*:

>Deep into that slot canyon,
>the entrance to Gaia's yoni
>welcomes this intimate procession
>of thinly clad souls.
>Each on our own frail tightrope
>of comprehension,
>with its fugitive connecting threads.
>A catwalk of steel spider webs
>offers the illusion of security,
>fond goal in today's perilous world,
>as we probe to define wilderness.

Pamela Williams work is a vibrant celebration of life's journey elevated to a level of wonderment, making it a meaningful exploration for those of us who travel this often perilous yet gratifying road towards self-discovery and liberation.

—Arnell Ando is the creator of Hero's Journey, Lucky Pack and Transformational Tarot and co-organizes Tarot history tours of Italy. *www.arnellart.com*

Preface

The Way In, and Through

A number of people have commented to me over the last few years that they had no idea I wrote poetry...so it's way overdue, I realize, to step up and share what comes through me. I could blame years in community where memory was a prerequisite, the endless rebellious resistance of my sixteen-year old self to my parents who were both writers, or I could speak of my history of wearing the muse's costume. While satisfying in its own right, I find a different truth and resonance with my own divinity in scattering my own stories along the journey. And then there's just the synergy of this juncture.

My writing springs most often from some deep emotional well, whether fueled by grief or wonder, or just the puzzles I'm immersed in of both the visible and invisible worlds. It's very experiential, as well as offering larger metaphor – so, if you've shared some of this path with me, I hope you'll recognize my laugh or poignant tears over a moment in time. If you sit with the work for a while, recognition may come, though perhaps of some archetypal wisdom of your own! The power of word is my gift to take you, the reader out of the busyness of life, to remind you of that safe quiet place within. It's an opportunity to take time to examine who we are in these shifting times and to look at that in the larger societal mirror. Some of my more recent work, both written and visual, has become more ecologically / politically tinged in that way, as in my recurring dialog with the bee – how can we not feel that collective impact? I offer by example in my embrace of my own vulnerability, a springboard for you to greet your own, and hold space for you to do so.

This outpouring of creative juice is supported by my Rosicrucian studies, my yoga practice and Tarot explorations, my chosen tribe on this trek, assorted examinations of modalities such as Access Consciousness, and my own version of Aries tenacity and endless curiosity. In each section of this book, you'll find diverse interpretations of the one word titles, intended to give you pause to pore over what may provide peace or exhilaration, or offer a platform for further analysis. Recurring themes on the path of this life push me to find new lessons, new ways of letting go, savoring, or leaping for the abyss. Embracing the laughter and holy moments and a deep fascination with transitions continue to carry me forward in this work. The title, 'Hair on Fire' comes from a Buddhist saying that we often don't do something until we must. I invite your slowing pace to fall into these mysteries with me. Please feel welcomed to share your findings as they emerge at pamelanow@yahoo.com

Light, Life, Love, and Shared Blessings,
Pamela Williams
2016

Hair on Fire   7

ACKNOWLEDGEMENTS

My endless heartfelt gratitude goes to such an abundance of supportive cast members that I'm humbled anew by recounting them.......to Stewart, for first seeing me as a poet, infusing me with that vision, and for the ongoing advocacy in that journey. To Dr. Sharie Liden, for loving more, and for giving me my first platform to put it out in the world, along with a lesson in setting intentions. To Robbie and Binda, my family, for always cheering me on, even when it's not my turn. To Jade Leyva, of the biggest *corazon* I know, who first introduced me to others as a poet, and who brought me to the wonderful crucible that is Tortuga Gallery in Albuquerque. To Rudy, for your lavish, honest, and insightful editing, and for so often knowing what I really meant to say. To Zannah Noe, for being such a brilliant and generous business cookie, full of clever promotional wonders, and for the timely graphics assistance. To Juan Wijngaard, for such kind willingness to share your wealth of experience. To Ozzy, for showing me the value and wonder of having my hair on fire. To *cara* Arnell Ando, for always looking for the next stepping stone to generosity and nurturing. To Joe, for showing me a new version of a muse and for talking me home to myself.

And to all of those who read about my project on Indiegogo, believed in me enough to make this book a reality, and helped to prove it through their generous sponsorship - particularly Robert Marks, Maeve Heald, Cloyd Hinkle, Olivia Ruiz, Belynda Webb, and everyone who gave something to show their support, and to the anonymous donors whom I hold dear.

Altars

In Planetary Time

Objectively, it's quite a time,
full of metaphoric thunder and lightning.
Careening planets,
colliding vulnerability and empowerment.
Deep breaths and girded loins
occasionally required
for the day's lessons.
Sometimes an inscrutable jaguar
appears in a coffee house
breathing his hot breath
on your hand
and bringing a message.
And some days a new nest
is in progress
on the back *portale*.
All joining in the weft
of this miraculous
sacramental cloth.

Ofrenda

My brothers and sisters traverse that river of grief today,
strewn with marigolds and tears.
I feel their drumbeat and chanting,
carrying us all through these passages.
Carrying me too, from afar,
as from our shared inception.
From Woodacre to Richmond seems not so far.
Yet encompassing such vastness, such distance.
Honoring Leona, ever a teacher.
Calling out names, Stephen and Jerry in one year.
The grand and more unfathomable losses
to our planet and our journeys' companions.
Our personal losses of innocence and hope.
Prayers that we may we find the strength to keep believing
in our shared goodness and love,
and the power that we are one.
I light my candles,
my own *ofrenda*.

Today's Buffet

The abundance on the buffet that is this day
stokes the manifested momentum.
The sweet staccato accompaniment
blesses the rushing current of our prayers.
Marriage on the woodland stage
set for this adventure,
blissfully joined with the cosmos beyond veils
that we cannot yet imagine.
What catalyst will appear
to foster such a union?
More love as fuel today.
Meditation, practice, trust,
all supportive friends.

Spring Vantage

I'm drinking in the lush greens of spring,
savoring each bud and gently waving newborn leaf.
Relieved to have noticed in the nick of time,
that the jasmine has begun to trumpet,
and the crepe myrtle is sprouting at last.
I watch the lawn chair vibrate against the spring gale,
on its sled base as are we all.
Seeing the analogy, the fluidity
of the current platform we teeter on.
I drunkenly inhale today's glass of fresh lilac blossoms,
fascinated by their pungency,
and grateful for their ability
to shoulder their way to the precipice of my consciousness,
trampling all other concerns to take charge
and remind me at least briefly what matters.

THE KEYS TO WILLOW STREET

I find myself falling towards my center
and yours,
willing to become lost in the magic,
in the deep seductive forest of your soul.
You offer up the gifts of who you are.
I am intoxicated by the array,
tantalized, and afraid of the honor.
I am afraid of what comes easily.
But challenge me just enough,
and the warrior in me will emerge
to dance with that fear.
Be wary of gifting all your power
to a headstrong woman.
You already hold my heart.

WE MAY HAVE HEARD LA LLORONA

We may have heard *La Llorona*
barely audible just beyond the ridge.
Mournful, as they always tell the tale
and with that plaintive melody of loss.
A moment's shiver in chorus with the noble aspens.
That vast silence in union with the rushing water.
And us building our own convergence.
Where were we? And what did that matter?
Truchas, Ojo Sarco, or just someplace on a curvy road
to the story we co-author?
Saluting the guardian dogs in passing,
pondering the evenness of that life.
The white sentry rises to honor our departure.

TRUSTING THE GNOSIS

The exaltation, the exhilaration of this gnosis
transports and uplifts me
to a more peaceful plane.
To the ultimate sanctum
guided by the labyrinth
of this life.
My *compadres* in this soul pod
reassure and nurture me
in the deep water of my fears.
The ancient wisdom
confirms the way
despite the fleeting nature of the journey.
Resonance repeats the song of the soul.

Witnessing the deterioration,
the demise
and the struggles
along the way
tests the resolve
of the truths.
Hold to that knowing;
cling to the glory that this is.

Wheel of Fortune

A hidden longing quenched in such sweetness.
Being cared for with the deep desire,
to build for me a castle of light and love.
Fragile frailty of our humanity,
wounded and vulnerable as we all are.
The wheel of fortune keeps me in motion now.
Promises of revival and redemption
giving me buoyancy through this turbulence.
Growing certainty of the magnitude
of this treasure, of this time.
Today, I hungrily snatch up the kernels
of understanding as they surface.

Redbud Infatuation

Mama, the redbuds are blooming.
They've upstaged every vista,
and they break my heart again every day,
thrilling me with each new sighting.
Each one a cousin to my childhood companion,
and each more intensely hued, I'm certain.
There are choruses of pink and white fruit trees, too.
I strain to name each one.
And there's a quince.
Can we plant a quince, where we nest?

New Here, Yet Again

This morning's stillness, startling and foreign
reminds me yet again that we tread this path solo.
A heartfelt thank you for the lessons.
No crossing of my path today, save that solar beckoning.
But the refrain remains.
Can't we find a hand to hold?
A tribe to affirm?
A container to tenderly cradle so many questions?
Sometimes just speaking them provides catharsis,
or provokes.
So many of us share the wonder.
Perhaps I hold out a key.
It could be true that you see my way.
That hand up the ladder of lights
is invaluable
and sustains me now

Neighbor

The toothless and androgynous elder from
down the road appears,
surveying the *acequia* from the asylum of a walker
and accompanied by protector dog.
Both greet me inquisitively.
A bit of a journey to the far reaches of the kingdom, I suspect,
and never before seen beyond their own property.
I wonder at the possible extent of its past,
thinking that the tiny abode next door
was a recent divestment.
The new owner proudly clearing brush
and dilapidated fencing,
eager to wave as I pass.
The smaller still ancient and crumbling adobe
compels me in wonder.
What stories it likely holds.
I find the soft green of the rickety window frames
and precarious door a charming classic touch,
wishing I had stopped to say so,
and perhaps to hear a story.
I wonder too, at the early model bmw
retired to the shadows.

HOLDING YOUR HAND

for Lisa

New tendrils and their most delicate of blossoms
grow patiently over the wound.
The tear in the fabric of your soul
that never completely heals.
The fortitude and valor that develop there,
from this recipe of pain and unfathomable loss.
Those who love you most deeply
would share how you are seen and held in that tender place,
transmuted into the wonder and glory
of who you have become,
the grace in how you show up,
heart first, always…
May the healing love that surrounds you
and the voice of your muse
buoy you aloft
and carry you to a place rich in serenity and dreams.

DUSTED

Curious, too, about the promissory gifts from the elements.
Observing from that sweet warm interior,
the abruptly slowing pace catches my eye.
Clad all in black, the examination easily at hand.
My subject raises his eyes to source
and smiles in humble gratitude for this sparkling endowment.
the gait now more measured in mindfulness.

Insider jokes include the signature dusting
always evident with the tribe.
But this offers premium magic,
magnified in the aura of each illumination,
and beguilingly inviting deep immersion.

Corrugated Cliffs

Reflections in the scratched glass.
Mirroring, awakening with the drama of dawn.
Tracing the sparkle of that corrugated ribbon of cliffs.
Mogollon, perhaps?
Noting this opportunity
for practicing
opening roses from this height,
if no longer from the perceived security
of this neighborhood.
Southern route to the north.
Remember the presence of the egregore.
And meditating on the phrase for shape shifting.
Yeah, that's how it happens.

COYOTE CASUALTIES

The coyote casualties continue
in breaking my heart.
A young one this morning,
the dear cost of this endless
rush to succeed in some elusive something.
And all amidst the clouds and mountain hues
that won't bear description.
If you were driving,
I would struggle
to capture them with pen or paint,
gathered, and held so tightly.
Treasured, nurtured,
as with that loving cup
to bless your day,
as your own spacious heart
blesses my own, still.

ALTARS

I think the bee is too big
my opinionated artist friend said.
I understand being opinionated.
But I answered, it's all about the bee.
Everything that we do can be an altar.
Each creation a gentle gesture of love
or a grand passionate one.
Paint and glue applied with adoration,
or the keyboard thoughtfully stroked.
An *ofrenda* in supplication
for our own divine gifts.
Prayers may come in the form of soup
or sutures for a wound
seen or unseen.
Comfort or currency.
It began as a series
as is all of this journey.
Today my prayer is for the One that we are
and for all that is softly laid on
the altar of this life.

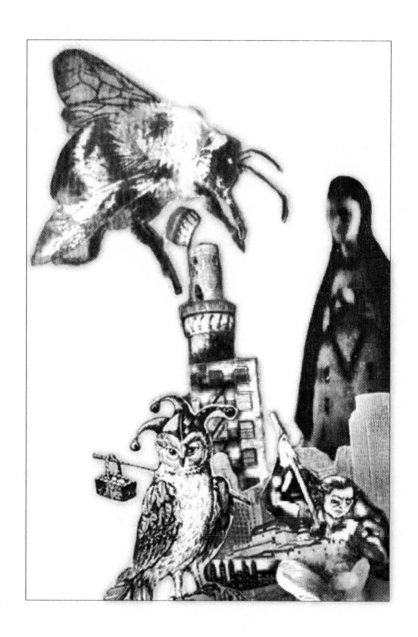

BALANCE

Knitting in my Dreams

My house redolent with peppermint,
an overture to the mouse king.
Ablaze with the glow of Imbolc,
in direct alignment with Persephone's passage.
Zealously knitting a new life,
even in my dreams,
and laughing at such grand metaphor.
Each cleansing, each pylon,
every small victory in conference
vouches for the veracity
of this course.
Homage to intuition
in restoration mode.

Entraining

As those first early tendrils
reach in through the gate,
a glimpse of a tall departing mast.
The passing ghosts salute me
in my ambivalence over the threats
of too big a dose of solitude.

We can't go back.
I maintain though, that we must consciously choose
how to move forward
and whose hand to squeeze
on the journey.
I pause in crossing,
entraining with the singing cables.
Memories flooding in,
blotting out the loop of questions
for a few verses, at least.
A practice, this moment.

The Next Rung

It's the same wrenching deep teal
of that Siena sky.
The one that we all struggled to capture
in memory and mobile device.
We spoke longingly of its nuances,
and tried to connect the stars
in much the same way.
Reaching always for that next rung,
while delighting over absorbing
the history.
Imagining the pounding of hooves,
the pomp of all that energy,
presided over by the stone *torres*,
sisters to the local adobe.

SELF–LOVE

In the ongoing effort not to disregard imagination,
I lovingly hang another piece of art,
conjuring more cozy rugs and forgiving cushions,
pulled up near the fire,
and fueling my own fires.
Then I imagine myself back on that bridge
to the next destination,
smiling the joyful smile of the fool's journey.
Reminder that sometimes the bridge itself
may be detonated by time or progress,
sentimentality over passages be damned.
The plethora of accompanying emotions,
barging through my consciousness
like passing cargo freight,
often as weighty, and gaining in momentum.
Now reverting to the focus on beauty -
treasured accoutrements of self-love,
and reveling in that knowing.

PLACE

Train in the distance
irrigation in my lap
and the lovely pond gives me pause.
Am I oddly a bit below sea level, here?
Truly an oasis I've landed in.
Couldn't have imagined myself
surrounded by horsetail, bamboo,
and koi with fins the size of my face.
A dance between stopping
to appreciate what I asked for,
and holding the focus on
giving what I can.
Meditating on both,
while sifting through the past.

What was Within

What was within, all along.
Now illuminated, owned.
Exposed as an offering.
The dregs of regret and sadness as fuel.
Reclaimed laughter a lofty goal.
The wistful moments
as a train passing.
And then with joy
I notice that in this glorious sunlight,
those sheltering mountains have become
littered with snow.

Softened Rebuttal

Having resisted that query so vociferously,
I smile over my own concession,
smiling more often, of late.
It's seasonally driven, no?
This need in a chilly and foreign world,
to curl up by the fire,
with inspiration, query,
the latest lessons to conquer,
or in pursuit of my own creation.
Marveling at the array of the coleus,
in startling contrast to the vivid and unlikely Spring green,
of that tree whose name I don't yet know.
Swelling drama of this last super moon,
propelling me into the robe of the priestess.
The successes of art on adobe, Fairfax and Firenze,
the resolve of the career in flannel sheets.
Remaining challenge of the grounding of stimulus.
Trusting that it too will fall into line.
Each day's small victories
nudge me to the next stepping stone,
and find me shrugging into more comfort
in these wings.

MELTING

Surveying the warm light emanated from within,
smiling at the momentary rose hued serenity attained,
buttressed by the rekindled yoga routine
and the afternoon's first assignation -
the prescription more than filled, for this day.
Melting the fear, the clinging struggle to not dissolve.
Reaching fervently for this reckoning,
while the practice of patience is revived
in the kiva communion.

Of the Color Blue

First in the stark relief
of black and white,
the day emerges through the cottonwoods.
Know the likelihood of that blue
that's been called headstrong.
It's the same one
that can represent the distance,
that can awaken the optimist within,
speaking in one of its assorted voices.
Listen carefully while assembling one's self,
while choosing which mask to put on,
or to leave off.
Today's reality show will attempt
to make you the star.
Competing agendas will clamor
for attention,
for center stage.
Hold tight to your heart center,
to your own firm resolve.
It is your circus,
and your choice of performers.

Just One Day

Only yesterday morning
there were fat buds on that tree.
They were hugging themselves tightly closed.
As a novice in local horticulture,
the ensuing explosion of blossoms
upon evening's return
could not have been more shocking.
I must attempt an introduction,
a conversation about ancestors,
and shared history.
Concerned that leafing too soon
could be subject
to that predicted latent cold snap
potentially even in May.

Then on this next morning,
marveling over the display,
I saluted three other kinds of blooming trees.
That's forsythia next door,
and daffodils underfoot.
Little new shoots,
hollyhock beginnings,
so many alluring mysteries.

By just midafternoon,
there were complaints of the increasing chill.
My technology did mention wind.
Suddenly the air is filled with flurries…
the heat must be prodded on again,
and then, snug at home, the fire lit,
honoring each fleeting moment.

Irrelevant

Are you holding your focus?
Firmly this side of the valley
between here and upstream thought?
Pinpoint exactly that spot between gratitude
for any job
and fear for its fleeting nature.
Exiled to that planet off to the side
of the cosmos.
Should you have any questions
regarding your path,
please consult your inner muse.
Irrelevant, many days.
Scrambling to find solid footing.
That perception no longer the norm.

I Met a Praying Mantis

I met a praying mantis tonight
Lovely, svelte, shockingly chartreuse, and serene
with her boundless alien eyes.
Frozen in the moment of my snapshot.
Not nearly close enough
for the sought after detail,
but clearly intrusive with my technology,
I wanted to see her indignant departure
in slow motion,
to study her wild and flexing gait.
A yogini in action.
And all inspiring of new reverence.
The welcoming committee
that I hadn't noticed before
in my rush to completion.
Now, with time spent observing the ants
conspiring their own empires.
A reminder that I must look up the moth,
and the giant helicopter of a beetle,
and whose scat is that?

Golden Light

We would have gone rambling
in this last glorious golden light,
hands and hearts brushing.
Attempts to assuage each other's fears.
Can there be a safe container?
One strong enough
to hold the demons at bay?
To give solace to that deep loneliness?
Before you've had a chance to savor,
to reread those lines,
the moment has passed.
And we're left alone with ourselves again,
facing our own shadows.

BACK–ROAD

It may be a dramatic one act play.
Some days competing dioramas,
or perhaps just my own reverie.
Keeping me company,
from a to b, and back again.
Offering the highlight of some.
A cartoon-like encounter,
with a coyote at full throttle
towards three of us incased in steel
passing the oblivious cyclist...
Sudden awareness of impending threat
causing an abrupt u turn,
paws smoking,
and retreat to the safety under the trestle.
Perhaps the favorite vignette?
The vast field paved with bobbing Canadians,
and flanked by its mirroring neighbor,
hosting legions of Lesser Sandhills.
On the berm between,
brother coyotes patiently meditate
on the buffet selections.

Awash in Blessings

The *portale* ablaze in the drama
of that glorious morning sun
blaring over the *casita* roof,
unimpeded by the stark naked branches.
I am equally awash in blessings,
teary over the riches of this path.
I pause, reflecting on the luxury of my warm retreat,
including its metaphors for insecurity and intrusions.
Rushing to construct new lists,
I can envision so very much.
The optimism runs strong, today.
It drives, and prods me
to the next rung, the beckoning process.
Yearning, longing, curiosity to unwrap more knowing,
all compelling to the work here.
Such a rich and ripe time
with this newly beloved friend
inspires and informs the trajectory,
affirms my belonging
on my way.
I treasure how reverently we both received the bounty
of each other's offerings,
our plates at once empty and full.

Litima

My favorite image is the tousled sweaty one
softened by exertion,
and sometimes too, by connection.
One eye squinting
but the gaze open and direct.

I am full and warm,
blessed by the lights and shadows
of what you bring.
Having felt the sweet sharp heat
of your *litima*,
I bask contented in its lee.

I continue, with indulgent smile,
to attempt definition, explanation, dissertation,
for those who search so hard,
and surrender, smiling peacefully
into the rare place without that need.

Few have touched me
in this deep and sacred place
as does this bridge builder, hand holder,
mentor, and carrier of my causes.

I know the cost of that,
and I am deeply honored.

ANOTHER

Another twenty-nine degree reading.
I would attest though, that it feels disturbingly far more frigid,
reminded of the term wind chill,
fled so long ago.
Or could I perhaps be listing twenty-nine degrees from center?
That's plausible, as well.
But mid-descent, I'm pulled up short,
by the crisp buttery new moon,
saving me again and again,
to shake my head and my sensibilities,
and to don a revitalized smile despite myself.
A potential crisis, fades in relevance.
Amidst what may likely be another reckoning,
some solid ground appears beneath me.
More and more frequent, it's noted,
with the bells of the hour less evident, now,
except in times of reverie.

ANCESTORS AND APRICOTS

A lone placid donkey
appearing, contented on his palatial hillside.
The meticulously manicured plantings,
like the tufted pastiche
of a Bedouin carpet.
It all exudes an unfathomable serenity.
They did not rape the land
with such savagery here.
Only the Sabines.

Having heard of hawthorn trees again
after so many years,
I muse over the delicately blooming saplings
that may be apricots.
The pride of a thousand years of ancestors.
A world to cultivate such brilliance.

Redbuds here, as well.
The synergy in that.
And burning to know these imagined woods
come alive.
Soundtrack of Italia radio.
The way to Capalbio and the sea.
Random leftover ramparts
strewn across the landscape.
Swords dropped and another Spring revealed.

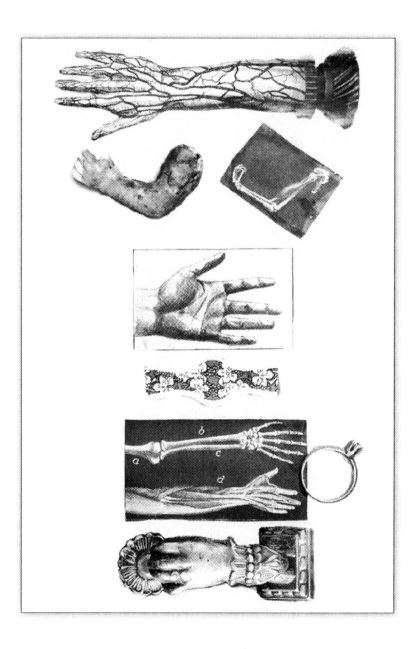

RECEIVE

Doorways

for Jer

Taken in through the doorway to that
glittering and mysterious world of opera,
not to love it, I admit.
Pieces of that came later.
But the awe, the thrill,
and watching such reverence for it,
make me wish I'd paid more attention.
Now, I listen to Paul Potts and salute you for what you offered.
And then I smile in memory of the stampede up the stairs.

Yosemite's magnificence, most of all.
Seeing the intricacies of nature,
so much majesty to experience,
all of the first time adventures on a shoestring,
and it really didn't have to cost city prices.
That was before I got hip to that possibility.
To what beauty and joy were available.
I thought I knew which train I wanted to board.

The sadness is for the unrevealed, and unexplored,
the passion restrained.
The hidden reveries of the poet's heart,
finally disclosed on my way out the door.
I vowed to ask more often for what I needed,
and paused, grateful, too, for the legacy of friendship.

Unseasonal Passage
for Boo, C, & J

I pause for a moment, abandoning the rose pruning
and the delayed shearing of the grasses,
musing on such unfamiliar solitude.
Missing that comforting furry presence
always craving shared warmth and affection.
How easy to take for granted what sustains us.
Metaphor he is, for all the love we carry.
Cathartic again for me now,
holding nature's hand
with the winter sun on my face.
But startling in this foreign silence.
I turn the music up.
Light the fire.
Find more candles.
Why haven't we always lit more candles?
And where's the safety net of a car always in the driveway
to guide me securely home?
The welcome harbor is within, I know.
But I had forgotten.
Lazy in love once again.
This new door opening for all of us,
and a bit too wide for comfort.
It beckons us to embrace an early spring.

Threshold to this Venture

From the netherworld of his nest,
the gypsy traveler cocked one eyebrow,
flashed a broad smile,
and posited,
Maybe you didn't need a watch.
Reminder of the enigma
of who will next appear
as the Zen master.
This, after the shouting had died down
over the failures of dispatch,
and after the plodding pilgrimage
from the default and undoubtedly dear
long term parking garage.
Now the bubble of imagining
slowly rises
with our turning towards the light.
Sometimes you can shake it and
it will do different things.
Did you know that?
And as an aside, it's sixty-eight degrees
in Milan.
Inconsequential that it may rain on this parade,
perhaps even a welcomed cleansing.
Eager to complete my vision of the tribe,
the anticipatory smile is ongoing,
while accompanied by reverence
for the swift passing of time thus far.

TREASURE

Ever richer,
ever more passionate,
the convergence of our two stars.
Even at a rare loss
to find our blessed common ground,
this feels like a new religion.
The stuff that defies my own belief
most of all,
surprising me every day,
jolting me with its intensity.
I discover in my lap
the power to move mountains
and create monuments.
These new and magical powers delight me.
I must pay attention.
Both of us.
So that we don't miss even a moment of this nectar.

SEASON OF ASCENSION

Deep breathing in this season of ascension;
mood elevation in tune with rising temperatures,
and inquiring new shoots.
This communion a reassuring rescue
from plummeting confidence.
Stepping forward into community,
sharing service and asanas,
both proffering a place of piety.
Circling above, the murder of crows
appears directly above home.

Review

Delicious reviving water.
I'm gulping every vista with such great glee.
You may have to go away for the veil to lift from the view,
and the lapsed delight over the reheated Fall color.
Rolling off my tongue,
Heart's Desire, Horse Hill, Issaquah Dock.
It's all right where I left it,
but refreshed, crisp and washed clean
in my absence,
as am I.

STEADFAST

for Christine

Ohh...
It hadn't occurred to me
that there wouldn't be sun today,
in a literal sense, anyway.
Another punch to the gut,
and somewhat like bumping
into a wound still raw,
and repeatedly.
For those of us
who insist on believing
in miracles,
this is brand new,
startling and unfathomable still.
Is this finality certain,
that that steadfast benevolence is no more?
I'm meditating on what a celebration
looks like for me.
I think it's a camping trip,
to a place where there are lots of stars.
We'll talk there.

THE POETRY OF MOTION

La Mesa, La Bajada.
Snippets.
Madera is just over there.
Treading lightly
through this peaceful thread.
Highway of many pilgrims,
countless journeys,
sacred mountains.
Debris from the Conquistadors.
Access the ancients out beyond Cabezon.
Mystical names like Golondrinas.
Secondary roads, *arroyos*.
All blanketing the serene respite from technology.
Outskirts of the country.
In contrast, too much structure in a pantoum.
To embrace a sestina, unfathomable.
Lag time, prediction,
watching the past recede.
Operating from memory as we must.
The Saturday Express,
with the evolution of words gathered.
Back stoops,
remembrances of Billy the Kid.
The golden orb appears.

My Own Benabbio

We had our soup in Grandmother's worn bowls,
offering prayers by candle light.
Our French roast in the Italian mugs,
imagining how it might be,
when we were actually in that realm.
We could never have dreamed it all, really.
Hit by an egg truck.
not once, but coming and going.
Could not have been more undone,
either way.
In between, grateful every single day,
even the hard ones,
because they were so few.
Imagine seeing and feeling, if you will.
All the time believing that you
wanted to hold my hand,
to be my shelter.
Believing in you, and in us.
Will you remember all that precious laughter?
It was just a little relationship.
And it was everything.
If you wanted it to be.

Marrowstone

for Stephen

I suddenly realized that my hands were still.
Not searching each other for focus or rough edges.
Here, I traverse quite different kinds of edges,
With a different type of courage,
that I find in some long forgotten file,
dusty with disuse,
but empowered by discovery.

The very young girl watches in wonder,
still new at patient observation
of other young, equally new to flight.
The edges I watch now are tree lines,
water surfaces and spider webs.
They provide the juice.
Always at unexpected moments,
and ripe with the urgency to be fulfilled
in materials yet uncombined and unexplored.

I joyfully gather a bouquet of feathers,
filled up with the sounds and the community.
The word nesting springs to mind.

LIGHTING THE CANDLES

Roasting potatoes makes it feel like fall
despite my resistance.
It's time to light the candles,
sliding into twilight, reflective as that can be,
in an attempt to suffuse those shadows
with a warm and nurturing glow.
The satisfaction of a day replete with blessings,
the small victories that sustain.
All this carries me downstream,
mindful of staying in the current,
lest the tangle of the shallows
slow this perceived progress in self-discovery.
Seeing the brilliance of daylight,
along with the fleeting lunar embrace,
remind me how I am loved,
held, sustained on this excursion
to a destination yet unexposed.
The emotions remain near the surface
while less often at unseemly times, now.
Still a hazard of excessive internal time,
and still the optimistic fool's journey.

I am Every Emotion

I am every emotion,
with glitter in my lingerie.
Selling smiles as a path to widespread peace.
Bathing the faux furry arachnids,
and minute rubber infants, ever underfoot.
On the lookout, always, for that laughter.
Still, I remain a bride here,
opening doors and drawers,
wandering foreign alleyways.
Climbing the hills,
claiming the neighborhood,
the work of gathering another tribe.
Some of them I recognize.
Welcomed, most always,
but with a still foreign discernment of my own.

Fall Gifts from the Jemez

Wild horses in companionable repose,
under a sheltering cottonwood
that seems to be dusted in turmeric,
and draped in its Fall finery.
The futility of deciphering the colors
of a distant mesa.
Then red, red, rust red buttes
enveloping me suddenly
from around a curve.
Contrasts.
Adobe on a double wide.
Gifts from strangers
making me aware of the promised embrace.
That roasting smell
not to be replicated.
The first autumn in memory
that didn't come too early.

DOROTHY COLLEEN

Living large, I've heard it called.
Being willing to go up on the roof,
or to climb into that tight dirty place,
to work harder than anyone I've known
to help your friend.
I didn't know that's what friendship looked like.
I'm sure that you're all here to teach me something.
Remembering to pay attention is the work.
And to know when to stop the work
and find the joy.
And to remember always how precious it all is.
How so dynamic a spirit, so bright a light,
can no longer be here sharing this path,
holding me up, and making me laugh,
mystifies me, makes my chest ache.

The undeniable truth?
There can always be
another storyline behind that dazzling smile,
that anyone may be sheltering demons.
And that more questions might uncover the grist
that moves us all forward,
richer, wiser, kinder.
May we all grow more awake and more aware,
while helping each other to find the way.

CREATIVE FIRES

I've laid a fire in the casita…
finding immense satisfaction
in foreseeing that moment
of instant response.
Immediate gratification
has always been welcome
at my table.
Longing for the fuel of the warmed
and passionate heart.
I smile in passing at the inception
of the next series,
spread in a beckoning display,
the majors awaiting this eager student.
Apollo overseeing my visit.
Mindful, meanwhile of the potential
for detours and roadblocks
accompanying the lure of the lessons.
Currently an *abrazo*,
of what the mysteries hold.

Corrales Respite

It's blissfully cool under the olive trees this morning
after last evening's deluge.
There was dancing in it on the restaurant patio
and even a snatch of song, I believe.
So much rich tradition hosted in that old hacienda
despite the affirmation of my disappointment
in their culinary culture.

This property is alive with its own vitality,
deep in commentary today.
The chickens have much to convey.
No doubt proud of their most recent offerings.
Such gentleness in that bunny
with the precious translucent ears
who seems to know how to share this peace
with the household dogs.

The resident roadrunner clatters in the background
Perhaps commenting on the quail parade rushing past.
Do you ever see quail who aren't in a hurry?
It could be a reminder of our own dialogue with time.
For an interval, all three dogs are still,
my new pack for a time.
I think about how we become family with one another.

Visualizing the desired slithering exodus
of that five-foot-long surprise visitor
met in the kitchen yesterday.
No regrets for not staying to see
the shape of its head.

Calling in Goddesses

Calling in goddesses,
trying on alternate costumes,
sweeping my own hearth,
owning my power again.
Wondering more infrequently
these days,
while sensing the arrival of my internal autumn.
I note that early pink glow gone in an instant.
I step over the shape shifting fear,
while reflecting on
the types of homecomings,
this one to myself.
Initially exposed, I thought.
Then warmed in my knowing within,
and claiming the metaphors of my choosing.
It is a choice.
And settled?
No, not a goal,
ever.

Below the Surface

The blood just below the surface,
in much the same way as the tears.
What catalyst?
What assault to the sensibilities,
the startling early weather?
At times, the merest breath of tenderness.
Hungry for that taste of the divine embrace.
Twenty-nine degrees
could signify either a location
or a digression,
a reverie or a comforting mantra.
Whimsy as a happy career move.
Don't imagine any semblance.

Baptism

The anointing of that persistent and pervasive sunshine
may tether me here.
The mysteries of this sacred ground,
with its chorus of ancients
and ever revolving fuel for display
of the manifestation of that work.
Marveling over the botanical synergy…
how is that moment in season
recognized and celebrated,
over and over, again?

A Matter of Course

Suddenly you see clearly for a moment.
Your neglect revealed
in all its naked shame,
and from the pinnacle of full glow.
Basking in how remarkable people can be.
Striving for kindness,
looking for ways to be kind,
kindness as a matter of course.
The logical next step.
It all began with the camel
on the World Market tote bag…
instantly awash in memories
and pain for what I didn't
share or do or offer of myself.
Please, please, may I get this lesson?
There couldn't be any finer examples.
Their names were Modesto and Crosita, little cross.
Six children between them,
twenty-four and maybe twenty?
Please buy Christmas for the children?
What else can I do?
Who else can I be?

Pumpkin Eggs

The color of a pumpkin, I swear,
and just swooningly delicious
to a foodie starved for superlatives.
Probably not much finer
than a farm fresh egg.
And imagine being acquainted
with your provider!
Respectfully, what is her name?
A fish was named for me once,
but she was loved to death.

Is there really a bronchial plague?
the more literal inquire,
and swearing some more,
I assure you that there is.
I've made my peace
with being so out of touch
with literal verbiage,
thinking that it gives me
different glasses to wear.
Filtering another mantis encounter
or the lesson of what a katydid is,
and yes that frog will come right on in
that open door,
reluctant skater on the glassy floor.

So, from the blackness comes the juice.
An expensive poem this is, then.
Tilting still towards worry,
the task list standing by,
while my self-care tests continue.
But is the pace of the monkey mind
perhaps just the least bit slowed?
Now what is that worth, really?

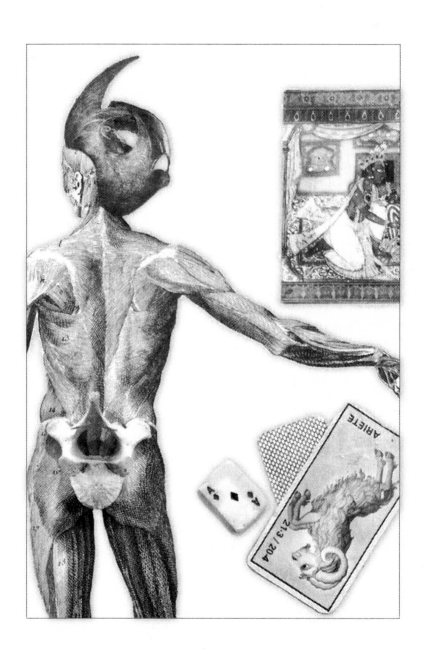

DISSECTION

FUGITIVE

I'm acutely aware of geography,
this voyage under microscopic examination;
shadows so much more obvious
from across the arroyo
than the ones I hold so dear.
But know that this view is colored
by my longing to see the acquisition
of that perfect peace and ease
in this migration –
that which is our birthright.
And I learn that it's okay to waver,
and empowering to be my own muse
for a change.
In this shining evening
I can grasp satisfaction,
enveloping me like hide and fur,
happy.

STUDYING POLARITY

Rumi reminds us how the shadow can dissolve,
as the candle becomes all flame.
Does it demand that sacred union?
Dissolution of some treasured self?
Always a proponent of enjoying one's cake,
is there room on the ladder for the warrior goddess?
A union of aspects,
friends and teachers, both.
Is the ecstasy embedded in the polarity?
Certainty that the laughter
resides precisely there.

Usual Fare

Thinking it was the usual fare,
I may not have measured my words.
And yet…
My gratitude is immeasurable,
my empowerment boundless.
The laughter becoming
delicious new daily bread.
Growing joy,
increasing intentions.
What gifts may be my rewards
for getting kicked out of my stupor?
Security?
And at what price?
I'm further amused to see
that there really isn't much to say
after all.
Have I really perhaps
done that work
all in the same day?

UNFINISHED CANVAS

Tapping on the side of that seemingly empty can,
aren't there just a few drops more of that Prussian Blue?
I was just warming up to work on this piece.
Never to be trusted with regulations.
The contradictions that we all are.
And it's a shade I never knew before.
Part of what makes me shiver.
Just a passing muse?
Inspiration for my own deepening practice?
Or something much, much larger.
The eternally young romantic in me
imagines that part all too easily.
Did you really say what I heard,
just as I was losing consciousness?
Mixed messages, mixed metaphors,
or simply a language I want to learn?

Some Days

Some days it's all just lists.
Do this; do that,
and scrape it out of my overflowing head.
An extraction process, if you will.
Maybe it's a lead.
Maybe it has heart and meaning.
Those plaintive coyotes as messengers?
First, locate some peace around the dilemma.
No shame.
And remember that fear means go.
Time perhaps to reread that book?
Or time to stop reading and leap;
embrace the risk.
Emptiness, foreign for a moment.
Searching for release.
Willing an end to the position of observer, analyst.
Searching for the courage to charge to the front lines,
to shoulder some of the progress.
I was there once before.
Maybe just on the wrong battlefield.
Did that war of style matter after all?

WISER

I've gotten a lot wiser, I think,
flashbacks of middle school aside.
Full circle, I recognize this crossroads.
Giggles, derisiveness, subterfuge,
even the note passing, I see.
And here we are still, striving to grow.
Moving in, moving on,
honey, I'm home.
The gratification of putting books on the shelf,
inspiration on the wall.
Blowing those cobwebs out the door.
What did she say?
Cutting away.
The nonsense and the outgrown.
Releasing the clinging fears.

RATTLING MY PERSPECTIVE

The cottonwoods have all changed their costumes
to shades of root beer foam.
And now here are mountains
that must know the same god.
Acquainted with the ebb and flow of any passage,
embraced and nurtured by this early rosy glow.
Flying into the light as we are meant to,
it strikes me that
the distance prevents us from knowing.
Metaphor for so much.
I would sit down and study
and inquire,
and ask for still more light,
to inspire and infuse,
throwing my shadow into stark relief.
And then just as I'm adrift in reverence
for those who so courageously ventured here first,
civilization springs up in my lap,
planted securely in the lee of those sentinels.
The klieg lights pour abruptly over the horizon,
bathing me in their heat, empowering.
Carrying me willfully, deliberately into the third act.

Reflection

That business of going to the edge, it appears,
doesn't always proof.
Some dances end badly, or early,
and some lives change color like these mountains,
reflecting what they've taken on,
and the new skins they've acquired.
Some days blur, from sweet to prickly,
transitions, without warning signs.
Sometimes just bittersweet.
Still, I endure, the optimist.

Two Stepping

New dilemmas,
new risks.
Opportunities to grow so much larger.
Larger in spirit.
Legacy.
Time to start drawing, maybe.
Coloring in the nuances
of that purposeful new life.
Am I prepared?
Are we ever?
Primed to dance with that unease.
Unfamiliar moves may be required
for us all.
Your move.

MYSTERIES

Mysteries.
There's this civility,
this waiting for the reply
to how you are.
Never known anywhere else.
Grave contradiction,
definitely not extending
to auto etiquette.
And most certainly
not to large trucks
with off-road accessories.
Same souls with different disguises on?
Are we so much of where we are?
What prompts the adding of new armor?
Or the larger question of what leads
to blithely shrugging it off.

FLYING INTO MY FUTURE

I'm in love again
with that instant –
the awareness of ascension.
Today beginning to peer
over the crisp crest of the Sandias,
as a myriad of golden pinpricks of activity
spring forth into this
fresh clean present,
ripe with opportunity.
Practicing possibility.
Flying so literally into my future,
and coming solo
as we must.
Shrugging search for comfort
in unfamiliar wings.
Grateful for the passing hands to hold,
and murmurs to calm the residual fears.
Realizing with a smile
that arrival has bought me
the gift of more time.

How

There are so very many of us
in the world.
How can we ever find each other,
find our rightful places?
The Sydney zoo?
That *gare* in Bordeaux?
A turn of the roulette wheel.
Can one soul truly stand off
a massive herd of stampeding cattle?
Pushing the envelope,
the only way to know.

Exposure

We all have our own locked doors.
Door to the heart.
Key to the kingdom.
Guarded oh so zealously,
lest someone see who we really are,
behind that veil between our assorted worlds.
Know what we really want to say
about what matters.
About the colors in a sunset,
the color of our dreams.
The romantic in us shamelessly exposed.
Vulnerably stripped of all our armor,
ironically cozy in its familiarity.
The artist, the writer, the performer.
Each steps onto his own stage,
in sync with a personal theme song,
and always terribly afraid
that we're not any good after all.
Who decides?

ENTRAINING

As those first early tendrils
drift in through the gate,
a glimpse of a tall departing mast.
The passing ghosts salute me
in my ambivalence over the threats
of too big a dose of solitude.

We can't go back.
I maintain though,
that we must consciously choose
how to move forward
and whose hand to squeeze
on the journey.
I pause in crossing,
entraining with the singing cables.
Memories flooding in,
blotting out the loop of questions
for a few verses.
A practice, this moment.

UNSPOKEN INQUIRY

The untried voice is always held responsible.
Being nice, being still, being good,
all proclaimed as worthy goals.
Yet it has become obvious
what price accompanies the silence,
and the weight of the mysteries that remain.
'I've always wondered what he was so angry about,'
my mother mused.
Despite my vow to be my intended bolder self,
I carry my own valise of riddles,
to be lovingly lifted up
in occasional scrutiny,
and then on a good day
reverently laid to rest.
Soldiering on, across this field,
there are the times
that we must just stop and weep -
both for our mothers who tried before us,
and for our earnest selves.

DOING THE WORK

Analysis fails to hold so much attention,
imagery and inquiry triumphing these days,
with their surges of delighted anticipation
and competing rewards.
Good, bad, right, wrong,
and ever, the taunts of those 'beyonds'.
Focus may be far less challenging
than always imagined,
in riding this swelling sense of certainty.
Know that the undertow remains,
while no longer such a looming threat
in this splendor of rising light.

About Arezzo

I honestly did not have an answer,
could not predict who I would be
or what I would need
in that world unimagined.
Would one more lost alley stroll
or savored aroma have sufficed?
Or would the pull of the next turn
in the road have beckoned
with a greater lure?
I wish I could have shared
how I saw your own need
to know and to hold
a plan in your palm.
Were you costumed as you expected?
Steeped in the mysteries
and prodded by the ancients?
Sometimes the journey
just isn't long enough
for all of the revelations.

MOTHER OF ALL PERSEIDS

Center stage lest we miss it,
that brilliant concentration of energy
plows a dramatic long furrow across our vista
leaving squirmy youth in awed reverence
and silenced giggles,
and all of us in our small selves.
The wake remaining longer than any others,
my own wonder tinged with that desire
to describe, to name,
to commit to visual memory.
How can something so defined
go untitled in the stories
of our lives?
I struggle to address its magnificence
by length and width,
sensing its unfathomable weight,
its texture defying my vocabulary.

I return to that dialogue on seeing versus feeling
and once again find them interwoven.
Reminded of the gifts and power of Moldavite,
I imagine this witnessing as just such a cosmic
endowment of the heart and spirit.

Could it perhaps counteract our cynicism
and bolster our compassion
for self and others,
reaching into our deepest inner realm?
Illumination and release
of our most profound longings
known and unknown?
Prayers that it be so.

LEGACY

Vestiges

Unaccustomed austerity,
prevailing proximity,
evolving flexibility.
A sense of humor required
along with warm socks
and the remedial
fire-building skills.
The street cleared,
the walk brisk,
that stream of duos slowed
to a winter trickle.

Projects abounding on both fronts.
Queued up and vying for selection.
No excuses.
Fueled by the temple drink,
the revolution could begin
at any time.
Affirmations,
the vestiges of what remains
forever imbedded in us.

Gaia Receiving

Deep into that slot canyon,
the entrance to Gaia's yoni
welcomes this intimate procession
of thinly clad souls.
Each on our own frail tightrope
of comprehension,
with its fugitive connecting threads.
A catwalk of steel spider webs
offers the illusion of security,
fond goal in today's perilous world,
as we probe to define wilderness.

The Mogollons spilling their bounty,
us traversing our teeming interior worlds,
humbled by the potential for rushing torrents
to threaten those massive steel bolts,
guaranteed for how many tons?

Just up the road
the world's largest shovel
works twenty-four seven
in the world's largest wound.
Yet the sacredness of this place
triumphs despite us and our
attempts at dominance.

See how we quantify and grapple with Nature,
our own submission so often the reckoning.
And then a little further north
in search of still more progress
we attempt to converse with
that vast external space
in which we float.

There used to be Balloons

There used to be balloons.
Skies full of their joy.
I can still come instantly
to total wakefulness
at the sound of their burners.
Now more of a rarity,
A luxury of a thrill.
We have to remember to search out those highs.
To be grateful for the gift, whatever it is now,
and to remain vigilant for the latest version.
It used to be that big booth order.
And what credit card will you be using?

Now, in this era of the Cardinal Cross,
there's still the random piece of art sold,
even the grand success of an opening
with the right artists.
Folks in search of pricey green chile jam
or coyote wind chimes
to embellish their travels.
And still the optimists open new restaurants here.
Tributes to our reverence for indulgence.
While not exactly on par with our former glory.

Three out of four of us at the bar aren't receiving any paychecks
And as the novice recipient of employment,
I stop often to marvel over that blessing.

THE SEDUCTION

Where would I begin
To speak of the gifts of this year of lessons:
of rampant green chilies
in the most surprising places.
But then you smell the seduction
of their roasting.......
The magic of the endless fluff of the cottonwoods
rivaled only by the second coming drama of the biggest of skies
And then you fill that vista with more balloons
than anyone could have extravagantly photo shopped.
My penance in the city of vision
grants my growth, in rockets of insight.
Would I have been so blessed,
in the neighborhood of my own selection?
How long, I wonder, until I noticed that always direct gaze,
with its sincere and solicitous greeting?
and the ongoing unfolding of possible futures?
Of significant others?
What of that?

The Big Kicking Belly Among Us
for Theo

Anticipating, impending, extending.
And soon to be giggling in our circle.
What joy in the welcoming of the newest traveler on this journey.
A new pup in the tribe.
Learning from Minette,
teaching us all,
new ways to see,
new truths to hold,
and to be held.
This inexplicably tiny burrito,
swaddled in so much love and aspiration
and wreathed in trust.
The conviction of a mother
for the rightness of this being.
Leaping confidently through the veil.
And soon to learn the father's magic,
pulled from other realms.
What juicy gifts await you,
precious and divine being!
Thank you for the reminder you bring
of all that is holy.

The Journey

You go along believing that you can see
where the road is going in the distance,
intention trumping logic once again,
while always alert for wildness
in the collage of hills and arroyos.
Remember that sudden grand leap of the mountain king
from the darkness of those woods.
Totem of possibilities.
And likely all too soon,
I'll softly close that door with a prayer,
no, two prayers:
one for your continued courage,
and one for my wiser self.

CHOICES

Overwhelmed, some days.
Which sage to read, and meditate upon.
What path the cards align.
and the looming force of the planets.
Can I touch those lessons?
Which archetype is speaking,
and to which of my masks?
Is this how growth looks now?
Or is it merely about surrender?
Passing perplexity that it may be.
The disorientation of this maturing.
At times we can only continue
to tango with these changes,
teetering on that precipice
of who we are becoming.
Today, the reverie can only continue
 in the Autumn sun.

SENTINELS

Sentinels.
Ghosts of another age.
Sometimes as simple as the dark specter
of the once lively café in the corner of the supermarket.
Now an abandoned cave,
waiting while executives somewhere
scratch their heads over what might make sense now.
We all struggle to reinvent ourselves.
With a start I realize that we stand witness
to the tortured demise of an era,
acknowledging in sadness those who have missed
the streetcar of awareness,
determinedly clinging to the tatters of their former lives
while watching the perks dissolve.
Those vacations, the RV and the second home,
all the fancy meals in sumptuous surroundings
surely will be ours again,
and then we can shop and redecorate
as though our due.
The gift of open space
with room to examine what matters,
what makes a life at the end of the day.

Risk Tolerance

I learned it while I was there, all those years.
Most everything in growth, in options.
In ways to see, to be, to relate.
The unbridled joy of those who came along behind.
Released, escaped from some ill-fitted past,
or so I believed.
How that unfolding appeared,
both before and after…
How to manage a burrito,
to embrace the luxury of sushi, the grit of the Tenderloin,
the colors and characters of the Mission.
Safe in the familiar comfort,
claiming neighborhoods as known.
The vast reach of my business kingdom
made me cocky, I'm sure,
that the world was mine.
Risk tolerance, they call it.
A journey so very rich in lessons.

Mandala

for Bry and for Margie

There was the sweetest house
called Mandala.
Rebuilt of hope and ancestry
high over Bodega harbor
so you could tell when
the salmon were running.
Visualizing the spectacle
of the lupine draped hillside
through the lovely spirals of the iron gate.
Special, from its inception,
tile laid with such pride.
Color choices infused with optimism.
Soleri's bells as background chorus.
Images of that kayak slipping into the bay.
Immediate wealth of memories,
mingling fragments of time.
My own bold silhouette remaining witness
to the passages.
Both Margie and the whale pods
soaring off the point.

Hollow Footfalls

Hollow footfalls echo
in this nearly empty shell.
Container for so much
laughter and pain.
Grand plans made
and abandoned.
Music and art stitched together
at the craft table, by the fire.
All nurtured by that pot of soup
from scratch.
Passing of a boyhood,
tall and taller still.
The creek and neighborhood
claimed and conquered,
Love, losses, lessons available,
while costly,
unlike the offerings on the curb.

HEARTLAND

Back here where it's all so flat,
the land cultivated to within
an inch of its life.
The view above spacious and full screen,
yet conspicuous in its simplicity.
It feels at once foreign and familiar.
The yin and yang of who I am.
The wispy sky stirred and feathered
like the icing on my cake.
I feel myself breaking open
with all this headroom,
with leeway to access my center.
Old crumbling tarmac highways,
memories drifting down the old fairways,
emerging at the weedy surface,
now stained with the tears.

Temperance

Irrelevant, it appears,
whether in sweet reverie over some tenderness,
or in anguish over the shock of pain's residue.
Spilling over as is likely
after being contained for so very long.
The eruption splashing onto my shoe,
and washing over my heart.
In that release, trying not to let your pain become my own,
the scales tilting just a bit
to the southern shadows each time.
Still I remember the joy first, even now,
while acknowledging its mingling
with the larger sorrows
for the loss of possibilities,
and for the extinguished innocence,
for both of us.

KUBUKU

What could Paradise possibly have to offer?
This is where the dragonflies live.
Nirvana music.
And they keep apologizing for the smallness of the room.
A bed in the garden, or a hammock by the paddies?
Vegetable curry that smells so sweet,
brought to your verandah.
First thing was lemongrass tea.
It would have been fine if that was our room.
I smiled at my first lizard.
What does a gecko look like?
I won't tell Laurie yet.
The music I will take with me.
Ceremony was a good choice after all.
Respect for our earth.

CURIOUS

Curious, the emerging deep focus
of a ten-year-old.
Rapt, and with queries
regarding detail and definition.
My best audience yet.
And then a gentle duet of wonder;
this one in a tender place
over the magic of the adventure.
Practicing staying in awareness
of opportunity.
A chalice, a fresh journal page.
A repository for joys and passions.
Today's lesson in animal totems.
Meanwhile, in another room,
disposable accessories from the mundane world
morph into mysterious and crackling survival gear,
all the while offering support for the gratitude practice.

Neighbor Girl

Willing to try any new adventure
as long as it wasn't fish.
Hell, she would have mailed chiles to me anywhere.
And they would have been cleaned, I smile.
But embarrassed, endlessly,
and then what did I change?
I *hate* the stuckness.
Spelling was not her forte,
but you knew that the word was mahvelous
and you believed that she was,
unequivocally.
Lots of days now,
I can do that.
Pretty fabulous legacy
don't you think?
Just always remain in the knowing
that this is only a moment
in your spirit's journey.

HUMBLED

Humbled, anew.
That ever-confident public face eludes me now.
Surely more accessible for some…
Gestures in Riola and Crestone;
an easier stance,
with intimate questions held at bay.
A more comfortable distance.
Space between you and the adulation.
No heart response required.
Too many opinions or inquiries?
Or too much easy laughter.
How to regret that,
or at least to soften the yearning.
What new context.
None imaginable but gratitude.

Wonder and Inquiry

for the tall boy

Once we pass that tower,
the display will unroll at your feet –
a jeweled carpet
of wonders to share
and adventures to construct.
Observing the metaphor
for the landmarks on this journey –
along with the reminder
to stay awake
and available to those moments of magic.
The fierceness of this age
mirrors the larger drama witnessed
of those in respectful chorus
with their land and their brothers.
The natural order.

To climb to the other world
of that mesa never imagined,
to commune with the source
of such careful reverence.
You can hold it in your palm
just as it holds the collective memories,
and as I hold you in my heart,
knowing that you will carry the questions.

HAIR ON FIRE

Unfolding

We speak of our wings
contemplating cellular growth
and firm footfalls on this path.
A new version appearing
still somewhat shrouded
through the veil.
Patience reigning
in some moments.
Swordplay on a windy day.
A hat and gloves comforting
while I bolster my ramparts
and design my interior womb.
Further unfolding forthcoming
spurred by the last departing
super moon
anointing me on my way.

TROUVE MEDITATION

Possibilities barge demandingly to the head of the queue.
Grist for building the *torre*, strewn across the floor.
How to convey the progress to which I bear witness?
The shifting landscape of our culture,
as of our larger world.
While the tower is in flames,
the mountain of knowing is being reclaimed,
one worn pebble at a time.
Re-emergence of the Divine Feminine,
the drumming Goddess,
wisdom of Isis.
With prayers that you always continue
the Sea Priest's steady beat
of the accompanying *cajon*.

Alchemy of Seasons

I brought out the wool comforter yesterday
and anticipated lighting that fire laid long ago,
abandoned to an early Spring.
A journey of just two weeks has delivered me
to a disparate world.
It ups the ante,
turns up the heat on all the looming projects.
Not necessarily a bad thing.
Eager for projection,
for application of that lustrous gold,
patience taunts me still,
while longing for the treasures of calcination.

Reflecting on that first Fall embraced.
Poignant in memory
and exemplary now.
It's in my fiery sign to resist
this time of percolation;
confronting now my need for expansion,
the push for publication,
alongside assorted closures.
Certain in the path of humility
and its promise of passions ignited.

Conundrum

The risk conundrum has reared up again.
Reminder of the familiarity of this crossroads
with its origins in ancestors.
Tasting the fears.
Smiling in triumphant moments of respite.
Ripe and novel with expanded certainty.
The value of asking new questions.
Loud acclaims of surging trust,
regardless of remaining mysteries
and boulders strewn,
and nights steeped in doubt.
Drinking in the beauty
through this new vantage;
recognition of this throng
and how it is different this time.

THE REINVENTION TOUR

Standing still this month,
chewing the elephant itty bitty bite at a time
Crossing lots and lots of things off of lots and lots of lists.
Still dodging other large beasts (and not always safely).
Legality looms.
Inertia threatens;
close cousin to total lethargy.
Legions of unsorted boxes salute me in passing.
Could they contain hidden wealth?
In fleeting sunny moments
development lures me.
Success in its assorted guises taunts me.
You know it won't look the way you imagine.
Know that, if nothing else.
Eyes wide open,
smile of eager anticipation in place,
put on your party hat
and leap for the abyss.

Prevailing Prohibition

The prohibition of tears prevails,
lest a collective meltdown occur.
Alchemical prescription
for future thriving.
Peripheral wavering
allows this work to proceed,
as the ballast continues to shift.
Fingers gently pried loose
from needs perceived as vital,
yielding to shrugging relief
at small completions.
No, you may not get back on the bus.
Seeming stabilization allows
for the spectrum of possibilities.
Very soon that last copter
out of Saigon
will deserve ceremony
and worthy sadness
at this crossroads.

PRECIPICE

Discomfort reigns on the precipice of change,
as the crowd jostles for position,
at the brink of the abyss.
Uncertain of allies,
and whether a hand to squeeze
or an anchor to offer
would provide any comfort.
It turns out that we're all harboring
some of the same fears.
Mirrors in those masks.
Choices in battlefields.

PATIENCE

Quarrelsome seems an apt description
A good fit with my own general peevishness today.
Old-fashioned words left over from Nan Bobbsey, I think.
Standing sentinel there, alert for questionable behavior,
ambiguous nuances, or conflicting agendas.
Doesn't it make you weary to carry all that armor?
Makes my teeth hurt, actually.
That painful metaphor of the guard dog
who feels himself chained to his designed post.
Friendly, even loving to those he trusts,
but shockingly aggressive
to any unknown or perceived threat.
Wonder what planetary alignment is suspect right now,
testing the depth of my resolve?

PASSAGE

We huddle here in our nest,
bewildered and fearful now,
of life and its abruptness.
I'm reminded of those fledgling birds
and wonder at the paradox
of becoming young and vulnerable again,
while sliding into the slippers of the oldest generation.
Sometimes the inability to fathom
each other's unease
washes over us as unpredictable surf.
I gasp at feeling new assault,
tender, without the accustomed sanctuary;
reflecting on whether I would go back to sleep.

Ongoing Transition

Sliding into the familiar rhythm of transition
brings a reminder of the potential impact of my words.
Reverence for the value of kindness observed
despite the pain,
the fears,
the height of today's hurdle.
That question of
'What will you do?'
raising unwarranted hackles.
Annoyance surfacing
beyond looming dark alleys.
Do any of us really hold that answer?
Hollow bumping sound
in the Spring wind
nudging us all forward,
as this perceived security
drifts out of sight
in our wake.

Particular Darkness

I send an extra measure of peace,
of deep and restorative slumber.
Knowing all too intimately
the fecund realm of that womb-like darkness,
palpable and so distinctly personalized.
A nightmare of a carnival ride
full of precipitous drops in altitude,
in attitude, in equilibrium.
Never predictable, never certain of much.
Then at last, with unimagined awe
and perhaps a sob of relief at the shift,
a rogue moment of sensing new truths,
of one's own strength and wisdom.
Impending rebirth and its healing.
Shouldering pick ax along with sword;
take up this new leg of the journey,
confident in the diminishing likelihood
of emotional breakdown on the street
or at the market.

MORE

More than merely the synergy,
more than that treasured resonance,
while vital as foundations.
The larger measure is revealed to be
how the distance is managed.
Whether tenderly cradled,
unwrapped as *furoshiki*, with kindness and wonder,
and held on that altar to growth -
or viewed in defiance,
heels dug in, sword wielded above.
Love of a good challenge
a potential ally in these times.
Though only the extant pearl of the project,
this gnosis a vanguard for the way forward.

Boarding

Boarding another time, in the ongoing journey,
while sensing that I've surely arrived
late to the platform.
Fumbling in my own twilight
for those missing parts
of who I believed I was.
Time now to cultivate strength,
meditate on inner knowing.
The practice of release continues.
Searching for words,
searching for meaning,
for my sword and shield,
in battling the abyss of darkness.

My tribe reaches out to me,
while I reach for the fragments
of my practiced self.
I weigh the prevailing urges
for creativity,
trampling other perceived roles.
Reminder to grab that famed brass ring
as it whirls past.
On some days, optimism and hope reign.
And others, I practice swallowing
bites of my own shadow.

Chainmail

Secretive, or disingenuous by habit?
Growing recognition of the appearance of that chainmail
and the cost of its weight
to both sides of its veil.
The covert and cryptic voice of the mystic
reveals itself again.
Shining light on the commonality
born in this culture of distrust,
bred in competition not subscribed.
Initially arriving as regal and respected;
in time emerging a despot.
Still the wisdom abides
for those loving pilgrims
delving deeply enough,
while treading softly in the inner sanctum.

Running

The kitchen littered with casualties
of the mouse wars
proves to be only a minor distraction.
Becoming accustomed to the ceiling
that's been pronounced ominous.
Running with the wolves,
my hair is on fire.
My spirit smolders with new contributions,
bubbling to the surface
and vying for my attention.
Boundaries require added vigilance these days.
There would be no remaining space
 for all this grand expansion.
Yet there appears a lure to find the access
to sharing this bounty.

KNOWING

Cleansing, anointing, preparing once again
to leap for that beckoning chasm.
Donning both armor and goddess finery.
Certain, this time of the way,
if not the look and feel of the journey.
Knowing finally, too, that you are there to catch me,
and wryly, that you always were.
Imagery swirling around me,
threatening overwhelming possibilities,
Targets, tangents,
transgressions at peace.
The cards reveal the unimagined,
in precise alignment,
synergy and stars.
Musing how the threat of such potential joy
can be so daunting.
While tenderly cradling
heart and soul connections
and how they exalt in return,
I awaken to the heights
of this solo voyage,
sojourner from many lives.

Relief

Relief.
A particular new piece of the vocabulary.
Different colors of relief
as with the various masks.
No interest at all in another;
bearing the weight of those already in place.
A stealthy retreat?
Unnoticed, amidst the surplus of beauty,
of wonder,
enamored as we were
in one way or another.
The pinnacle, it seemed,
After the endless, giddy anticipation.
Was it some spectacular descent,
culminating in fear or horrors unimagined,
or only that I voiced my own pain?

KINDLING

Grateful for the kindling offered up
for this pyre to joy and divine inspiration.
Molten activity expanding
to fill this new amphitheatre,
to stretch these wings.
Details always within reach,
chronic choice of pathway noted,
with its effortless declarations.
Cream, and matte,
and which voices will be welcomed
to the table.
But now,
the vinyasa reach extended
by this sanction,
and the fool's terrain a welcoming vista,
the pace accelerates in restless fervor.

About the Author

Pamela Williams is a poet and visual artist also doing commercial copy writing, with a jewelry design and metalsmithing degree from Indiana University, and a lifelong habit of artistic expression. Her grounded upbringing in the heartland provided the springboard for thirty expansive years in the San Francisco bay area, where the vibrant culture, spectacular geography, and her antique and collectible business, Pastense, all offered an endless parade of provocative fuel for her art and writing.

The extreme contrasts and rich history of New Mexico are now providing further vast alchemical inspiration and empowerment through its proffered seductions and mysterious remnants of a multi-cultural heritage, feeding her current assemblage work, development of her Etsy shop, NextSegue, and this first published collection of poetry.